D1593440

# *a*

by  Sophie Robinson

*with a Foreword by*
*Caroline Bergvall*

*and an Afterword by*
*Diane Ward*

TRENCHART: Tracer Series

*ƒ*
LES FIGUES PRESS
Los Angeles

Edited by Les Figues Press
Designed by Janice Lee
Printed in Michigan

*a*
FIRST EDITION

ISBN 10: 1-934254-10-X
ISBN 13: 978-1-934254-10-3

Library of Congress Control Number:  2008912181

Les Figues Press thanks its members for their support and
readership.  Les Figues Press is a 501(c)3 organization.
Donations are tax-deductible.

This project is supported, in part, by the Los Angeles County
board of supervisors through the Los Angeles County Arts
Commission.

Les Figues would like to acknowledge the following
individuals for their generosity: Johanna Blakley, Diane
and Chris Calkins, and Coco Owen.  Special thanks also
to Caroline Bergvall, Diane Ward, Vanessa Place, Susan
Simpson, Ken Ehrlich, Saehee Cho and Janice Lee.

Distributed by SPD / Small Press Distribution
1341 Seventh Street
Berkeley, CA  94710
www.spdbooks.org

TrenchArt 4/4
Book 5 of 5 in the TRENCHART Tracer Series.

**LES FIGUES PRESS**
Post Office Box 7736
Los Angeles, CA  90007
323.734.4732 / info@lesfigues.com
www.lesfigues.com
www.lesfigues.blogspot.com

For Aerin Davidson

1985 – 2007

with love

xxx

# Foreword

It is too late. Everything has stopped. Now all will be
laid out. Yet this is not what happens. This poetry is
elliptical, evasive. Its lines of thought and emotion
are sparse, broken up, they seem nearly unfinished,
as though suspended. The photographic details that
intervene throughout are fuzzy, seem to both wish
and refuse to allow for recollection. The series of
collages that close the volume keep both text and
image at a distance, at mind's length. It is through
the opening dedication that the volume is given its
coherence, the elegiac *raison d'être* of these insistent
refusals: the first letter of the dedicatee's name starts
with an A; then comes the shock of two dates: birth
and death, separated by a dash of barely 22 years;
followed by the moving, unspoken line of "xxx". This
*a* is a work of mourning. Angry, torn, hardly daring
to remember, yet shaped fully by the cruelty of love's
loss. Absence inhabits the many gaps of this painfully
detached collection. All in all, this first full-length
volume by English poet Sophie Robinson presents
her as a poet whose material handling is both lyrical
and performative, and structurally attuned to a mixed-
media presentation of her writing. Her segmentations
and obliqueness claim Stein's cubist presentness as one
antecedent. The volume's first part, INTERIOR, opens
with a photographic detail: that's a door or a window,
a wall, some plants or shrubs, outside, perhaps. Once
the verbal material starts up, it seems forensic, a
capitalised list of clothes and objects, brands of make-
up and creams, abandoned female apparels, false
eyelashes, mentions of ruptures, yearnings, lovers'
pleasures duly noted and removed for erotic pleasures.
The second part, GEOMETRIES, is an attempt at
ordering memory both as text and as photographic

image. The textual material finds its spatial logic by replicating the square shapes of the animated photo sequence of a young woman, raising a hand over a surface, the darkness of the palm seems to grow with each scanned image. Its third part, DISORDER, has as its epigraph a line by Francesca Woodman and brings to mind the American photographer's melancholic, ghostly work and short, ill-fated life. It works as a series of small collages, some bear the marks of stitches, hand-written notes, layered texts alongside cut-out images, interiors, perhaps. As hinted at in the work, Robinson's expressed and explicit difficulties in finding shapes and substances to her mourning, to effecting her act of memory, her painful and oblique or distilled account of love's brusque impact must also be read in light of the love that dares to speak as queer, its persistent social opaqueness, its mental duress and representational in/visibilities.

Caroline Bergvall

London

*a*

# I: INTERIOR

*the eagerness of objects to*
*be what we are afraid to do*

*cannot help but move us.*

- FRANK O'HARA, 'INTERIOR (WITH JANE)'

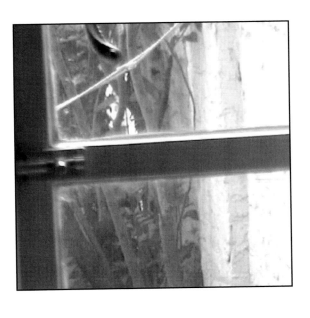

GREY STRIPE TOP W/OUT SLEEVES
cut off & out it move alone to the last it cry with gunk.


BLACK & WHITE STRIPE TOP W/SLEEVES
To really smile to forestall existence to grow and birth
to shake and be loud to take refuge.


BLACK CROCHET KNIT TOP
Fates hidden in the wind, being oneself, singing w/
impact choking & devouring.


BLACK SHORT-SLEEVED TOP W/BOW
Denim recognises itself in the night living in the
wilderness living under chaos living as the opposite
of fashion w/a quiet heart.

TESCO 3-PLY TISSUE
slope like that it learns to fit my finger to slide my
finger to soften on bones to kiss to the tip.


DARK GREY DRAINPIPE JEAN
an outwardness a ground teeth on teeth you loved;
breathy intake or some wet.


KNEE-LENGTH POLKA DOT SOCK
My shoulder playful and turned away toward the lake
between your knees.


NIVEA SENSITIVE HAND CREAM
Prune-child ashen in the sun in the day in the late
afternoon or early evening at dusk by the window
or just outside or far away with heady scent and so
pointed and so cold; or, an automatic squeeze a
mechanical gesture.  Jerk.

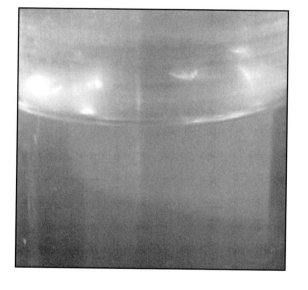

FINE-TOOTHED COMB W/HANDLE
My obtuse love left behind.


MEDIUM BRISTLE HAIRBRUSH
My obtuse love left behind, on jumpers.


MAROON LEGWARMER
Where are you gone quick and cruel.


LILAC SINGLE BEDSHEET
Jerk.  Sticky.

THREE-WAY BEIGE BRA
Cruel.


TOOTHBRUSH
A cherry split end a peachy a cat a remorse a
dreadful glee.


BLACK BOWLER HAT
A hazy a rounded corner a complex a bowling alley
every every a film of the ocean full of my full of spider.


BLACK LEATHER GLOVES W/BUTTON
Coins of unlust, artificial skin, staff layoffs, empty
eyes, stout and trembling alcoholics, infinite desire.

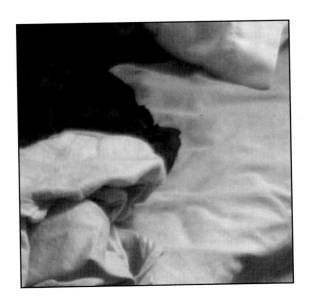

LARGE BLACK SUNGLASSES
Cobwebs, never fully, slit, kept, spindle, bulb.
Yearning.  'Out of an eye comes research', out of you
come a rupture altered all.


MAC CANDY BLUSH W/APPLICATOR
Down down down down down.  Involuntary.


J17 HARLET LIPSTICK
Plum or painted drawn out or on disappearing -


COLGATE MINIATURE TOOTHPASTE
Defining as pronoun an artificial divide on mine a
ribcage,

BLACK RIMMEL MASCARA
masses who kiss & wave & bop;                    you.


BROWN BOBBI BROWN MASCARA
A guilty lip rooted to the tip a drunken intimacy.


SPECTACULAR FAKE EYELASHES
A gentle pretext required.


_blue_

AZURE BOURGEOIS LOOSE POWDER
An apple of hope, the guarantee of a good time,
standing in fear of being hunted then moving busily
just out of view & faded.

14

DESK

taciturnity              like we always fight against
                    lang you hate to admit            sum

up empty              shell w/out
                    breath.


MORNING

Reckless t*ward            ?            [fragment]


ROOFTOP

To rooftop to rooftop to rooftop to rooftop to rooftop to


CUL-DE-SAC

A tilting envy – dawn unwanting – above & beneath
– chewy chambers intens w/anxt

## GLUE
A mania in church a lucky graveyard rider 30 happy
days.


## PHOTOFRAME
Faker faker fade onto whiplash crush underfoot a
thorn floating in cream


## LABIA
Tincan lover spraying on brick & plastering over the
messier ones.


## SUNSHINE
Clogged up w/puss & lifting off & pissing * all over
the quiet time.

LIPSTICK MARK ON MEDIUM MUG
Losses what we losses remember losses all over
losses ourselves.


FINGERPRINT MARK ON WINDOWSILL
Did        you        feel        trapped.


BLUE-TACK STAIN ON EGGSHELL WALL
The movement of sky.


LOOSE HAIRS ON MEDIUM BRISTLE HAIRBRUSH
Tender & unstable.

SMALL OUTAKE OF BREATH AGAINST BEDROOM
WINDOW
Molecule upon molecule


FEELING PULSE QUITE FAST THROUGH BLACK
JACKET SLEEVE
Evry      body


TODAY
Bound to its own destruction.


NOTHING

II: GEOMETRIES

*picking, pecking at*        *our skins ghost or angel*
*sent to tell us what*             *we didn't want to know*

- KATHLEEN FRASER, 'WING'

The upright nature of a girl, belied by
formless whirrs, signs of visible lust like the
density of skies, & the disappearing hour;
I think of you urgent & weak walking beside
billboards, missing out, flaking off in the
silence between 2 traxx, no tender riot
in yr geekheart [spliced open & pulsating
in four different places whilst the summer
is blaring musty and lithe, awful shiny
skin & sick tune of birds germinating light
as a new kind of loudness] & the crude urban
cosmos misses you & is just passing the
time w/dirt & money & pouting in the
corner w/out your nocturno-suspicious lure.

Multidigit spectators are writhing on the carpet longing for autumn and sanity, & metallic organs are wipe-clean & can be oiled & my phone can be dropped in shock in the middle of the street & will carry on working & there is soil in yr lacy frill & blood's like jelly these days, time loops around itself in bold & able gestures as I wonder around the Payless on Roman Rd & think of you grabbing my rarely thinnest hand & dragging away from jealousy now hardened now lain on a fridge putrid w/pollen & fashionable lipstick & you & you are made of dust.

Juvenile concealer upon ill-fitting victim status CUE I rise to say that my heart is only irritated OR a machine made frm human bones and a camera, but we eat camembert & memories here, not brains, so take yr spider, my dusty angel, & go back to striving for a city's tender shit, with a liver to match, kneeling beside the rubble beside the river in a funk full of mute & ache & vodka, & w/ the feet of a bird like tilt away frm the interpretable world & warble bcaus you never call me anymore.

This our night, hands clasped on the last instant it saw to the skirt, jump up & clap in a second, their eyes met over the pond in that lean death of words, that stagnant lang of stirring, that ground glitch or near touch that gleams & scarce makes contact before singing in the wind away from "how pretty you are" & all that blood that dances so, & now we all have our own rooms to not touch in, little slips of things w/vomit to spew on cushions & my bed is mine alone & yes didn't the cautiousness of human gesture surprise you? We cannot do it anymore, our own hearts exceed us.

Beauty is nothing is nothing is a gently disgusting residue of all that burps and smiles & life is terrible & holds back & swallows itself whilst 25 birds that might've perched on your arms&head can now fly in expanded air and yeah the autumn's going to need you w/ head like a broken toy & got no stable 'i' got no stable now all is fluttering around & the boredom of death O how we breathe you out like blah sad & longing for an airy exchange amongst urgent squeaky-clean majorities & CITY BOYS those smug wankers we put them in the margins.

The sheets on the bed are doubly broken
open & we contemplate the value
of silence, of being older, of 6
carriages derailed nr Bethnal Green where
you didn't live, & now strip me to the
joints I'm ready for that inky graze that
needle, 'cause we are young & live in bricks
outside of class & so nothing stormy
lifts in you & we cannot taste ourselves
& yr full of feedback when placed flush on
the hopes of objects that disintegrate
the moment of action to jump-shots
& wire & fluid, bt a doll is a doll,
however anatomically aroused.

Due harm has been done to our stardom & circumstance has rendered a dense scaffold of girls w/one helpful boypal & a vasospasm (problematic) & a vasospasm (undercutting) & a place where healing is bleeding a precious cleave & coiling branches & pulse & eyeball & dense platinum heavily nebulous & itching in the suburbs of my brain are all these moments bloated w/ritual & am forever shelling peas on the sofa w/you half out the door in a backwash of subjectivity, banishing 'culture' w/its sensation & movietalk.

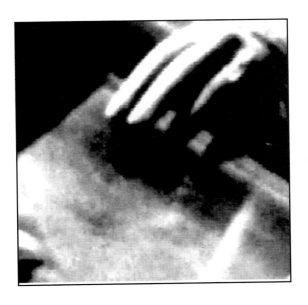

Invasive surfaces are cut cut in or out of hospital w/its dollars & chemicals w/humanity all Xeroxed out of view & shhhhed hideously, & do you remember our domestic serenades, my always-right pussy? I crave ashes & the upside even on these caramel-couloured Thursdays w/their functionalism & inflammatory TV sewing tears & beads of sunburn into the couch & all of this dubbed passivity you've left me with & these tiny endings & needling guilt, an athlete's fear & a parasitic twitch a loss.

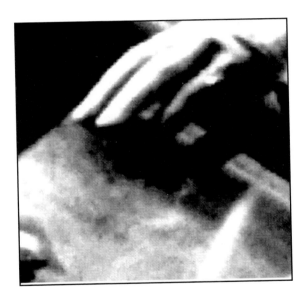

Prizing open the mechanism of
another's identity you lapse
& angst towards the vase towards the punk
the stereo & daddy's ideal needs &
Susan Sarandon is blaring telling
us to care more & that she'll see us on
our dream dates as if Baudrillard wasn't
watching & we really could eat sundaes
& not think abt our bodies & how we leave
details of them behind & slump into
the artifice of the daytoday, 'just
for now' we're blinking against the Tesco
neon & all those screaming heads tht can
really see the jewelled past smashing.

the      literary      real,      swollen      w/myth,
a    glass    downpouring    a    shard    a    fleshy
*we      are      different*      an      unavailable
profusion    creeping    between    us    a    groan'd
body      w/6      different      perspectives      &
every      body      is      passionate      &      drinks
lemonade        lying        around        w/girl
trying    to    say    &    lack    insight    what
&    my    cigarette    touched    the    sky    the    sky
a    bulk    of    yellow    dampness    neatly    com
pounded    for    all    this    eternal    progression
&    banner    'love    is    a    gesture'    TOUCH    ME
HERE   we   are   supposed   to,   firm   beneath   chest
& what late moon all unknown all just light.

III: DISORDER

*I wish Stein was here to shake me and kiss me.*

<small>FRANCESCA WOODMAN, UNDATED NOTEBOOK ENTRY.</small>

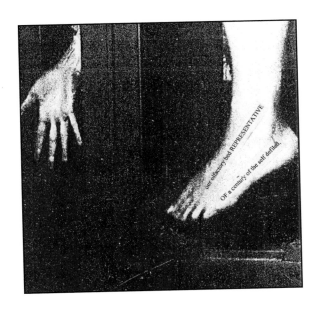

an influx of stallions & air around

you like an amputee

[AIR is the language

that disappears]

queer poeti
disenfranchi
sexual subj
shackles of

embra
gender.

nestness, enthusiasm, fanaticism, fervency, fervour, fire, gusto, keenness, militancy, passion, spirit, verve, warmth, zest

▷ **Antonyms** apathy, coolness, indifference, passivity, stoicism, torpor, unresponsiveness

**zealot** bigot, energumen, enthusiast, extremist, fanatic, fiend (*informal*), maniac, militant

**zealous** ablaze, afire, ardent, burning, devoted, eager, earnest, enthusiastic, fanatical, fervent, fervid, impassioned, keen, militant, passionate, rabid, spirited

▷ **Antonyms** apathetic, cold, cool, halfhearted, indifferent, lackadaisical, lacklustre, languorous, listless, low-key, sceptical, torpid, unenthusiastic, unimpassioned

**zenith** acme, apex, apogee, climax, crest, crowning point, height, high point, meridian, peak, pinnacle, summit, top, vertex

▷ **Antonyms** bottom, depths, lowest point, nadir, rock bottom

**zero** 1. cipher, naught, nil, nothing, nought 2. bottom, lowest point *or* ebb, nadir, nothing, rock bottom

**zero hour** appointed hour, crisis, moment of decision, moment of truth, turning point, vital moment

indifference, lack of enthusiasm, loathing, repugnance, weariness

**zing** animation, brio, dash, energy, go, (*informal*), life, liveliness, oomph (*informal*), pep, pizzazz *or* pizazz (*informal*), spirit, vigour, vitality, zest, zip (*informal*)

**zip 1.** *noun* liveliness, drive, energy, get-up-and-go (*informal*), go (*informal*), gusto, life, liveliness, oomph (*informal*), pep, pizzazz *or* pizazz (*informal*), punch (*informal*), sparkle, spirit, verve, vigour, vim (*slang*), vitality, zest, zing (*informal*) **2.** *verb* barrel (along) (*informal, chiefly U.S. & Canad.*), burn rubber (*informal*), flash, fly, ...

▷ **Antonyms** ... appositeness, inactivity, languor, lethargy, listlessness, sloth, torpor, ...

**zone** area, belt, district, region, section, sector, sphere, territory, tract

**zoom** verbal ... (along) (*informal, chiefly U.S. & Canad.*), burn rubber (*informal*), buzz, dash, dive, flash, fly, (*Brit. informal*), hum (*slang*), pelt, rip (*informal*), rush, shoot, speed, streak, tear, whirl, whizz (*informal*), zip (*informal*)

form against my own who screams

a large-scale projection of the female

w/ the taste of flowers in my throat &

**Z, z**

comical, crazy, *formal*), kooky *ang*), madcap, *ormal*), wacko cky (*slang*) 2. nedan, jester,

**zero in (on)** aim, bring to bear, concentrate, *pinpoint* (*direct*, focus, home in, level, train

**zest** 1 *appetite*, delectation, enjoyment, gusto, keenness, relish, *zeal—zing* (*informal*), SPARK, savour, tempo, et, kick

she screams w/

disease & time & nothingness

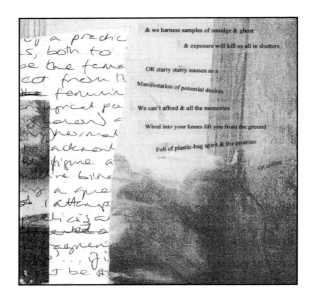

& we harness samples of smudge & ghost

& exposure will kill us all in shutters

OR starry starry nausea as a

Manifestation of potential desires

We can't afford & all the memories

Wired into your knees lift you from the ground

Full of plastic-bag spirit & the promise

Of coffee

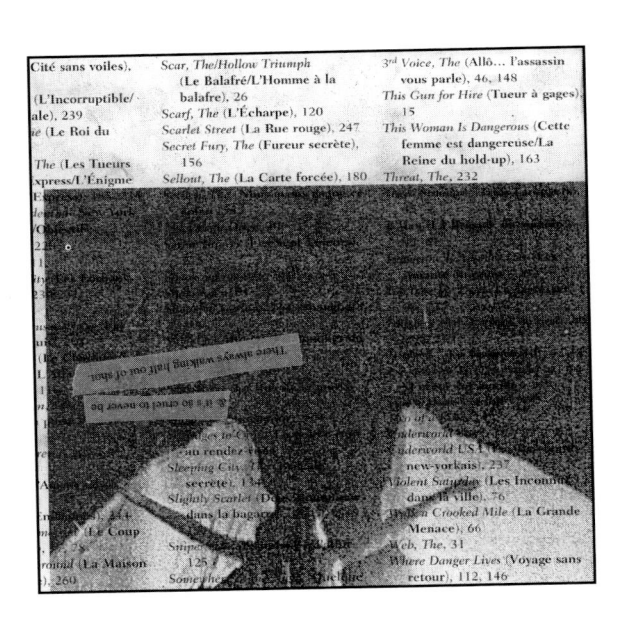

# Afterword

**What is the use of language
when there is death?**

"Oh! Leave... us
on this word
— which mingles
the two of us
together
— unites us
finally —
    for who said
it
       yours)"

                 – Stéphane Mallarmé,
                 *A Tomb for Anatole*

Sophie Robinson's *a* is not about death, nor is it about the dead. It was written after the loss of a loved one but it is not an attempt to enshrine nor to honor that person. In its fragmentation, its new beginnings, its non-endings, it is a document of a process. Death is the most undeniable disconnection; a threat to a survivor's sense of self. *a* is an exploration of that self and its tentacles, its collaboration in the passing of time and the physical world. It is composed of three formally distinct parts that all consistently examine a shifting cacophony of absence. *a* delineates a shattered world and is comprised of fragments of that world, the ground on which it rested, as well as all the places between. This fragmentation accommodates multiple experiences of place and time; it also reproduces itself until it is the act of fragmentation, not the result of the process, that speaks loudest.

Mallarmé's fragmented notes following his young son's death are an attempt to arrest death, to circumscribe its place in time by the act of writing a poetic 'tomb.' This was to be a non-religious resurrection of the dead, a flipping-off of death. Mallarmé's conception, however, was never realized (Auster). Rather than being an attempt to reach finality and understanding, the point of Sophie Robinson's conception of death is its inclusion into a continuum. The goal is not to stave off death but to trace its spreading: there is no moment when it wasn't and no moment when it will not be.

> **What is the use of self, what voice can speak, when there is death?**

"Oh!"

Mallarmé uses this word when language fails. It is breath's sound, incomprehensible, it clings to the living in a willful act. Robinson does not place the burden of incomprehension on language. Her "O" rises to death's occasion, stands beside it and sways:

> [. . .] & got no stable
> 'i' got no stable now all is fluttering
> around & the boredom of death O how
> we breathe you out like blah sad & longing
> [. . .] (34)

In *a*, she allows the loved one's objects to occupy a language-ridden space; her own grief to erupt up through the safety of the sonnet's formal lattice; and she allows language to become object through collages of printed words.

***What is the use of images***
***when there is death?***

In image and in language, *a* contemplates the ghostly interstices that persist when objects lose their handler. This book of left-behind voice, of human-held camera, of a dis-anchored triangular world, plots intention along memory-paths but has no concern for departures or arrivals.

It is extra-terrestrial and it is in the moment.

*a* is a project undertaken after the sudden death of Robinson's friend, Aerin. Robinson spent a day filming the empty studio and its objects that remained as they had been on the day Aerin left, for the last time. *Tender Buttons* influenced the writing in the first section, INTERIOR, that documents these objects in a Stein-like exercise, separating them from their terrestrial uses and meanings. Stein was interested in creating a relationship between the 'word and the things seen.' In Robinson's *a*, a ghostly lipstick mark projects itself onto a narrative of loss and a meditation on loss's elusive 'place':

LIPSTICK MARK ON MEDIUM MUG

Losses what we losses remember losses all over

losses ourselves. (18)

Like Stein, Robinson depends on objects to be a launching point for language. In Stein, the objects' ". . . reference remains central to her project even if representation does not. . . . [Stein] does not give us an image, however fractured, . . . ; rather, she forces us to reconsider how language actually constructs the world we know" (Perloff).

66

Unlike Stein, Robinson is not showing us how a world is constructed, nor is she attempting to deconstruct one in order to grant life to its component parts, to let them inhabit contextual spaces that have been denied them. Robinson's project is to document a world that persists while it is ceasing, inhabited by what is there and not-there. She has no control over this world's events and yet she finds herself playing the roles of both subject and object.

CUL-DE-SAC

A tilting envy – dawn unwanting – above and

    beneath

– chewy chambers intens w/anxt (15)

Robinson knows her language will not sate that which no longer claims hunger.

GEOMETRIES, the second section of *a*, is written in sonnet form. The still photos interspersed throughout, trace a simple gesture—"love is a gesture"—a woman, her features kept largely out of the frame, lifts her right hand and reaches out. The photos arrest the act of reaching out, their self-contained component-parts continually frustrating any climactic finish—they only allow "not yet."

            [. . .] & my  bed  is  mine
alone &   yes   didn't  the  cautiousness
of  human  gesture  surprise  you? We cannot
do it anymore, our own hearts exceed us. (32)

In contrast to the objects in the preceding INTERIOR, the object of the gesture (is it a final touch or resting place?) is not allowed to participate. GEOMETRIES is, instead, all about prolonging desire, nurturing life's place alongside death.

The third and final section, DISORDER, is a series of sepia-toned, word-and-image collages. They are dream-like, comprised of layers that seem to float on top of one another rather than masking what is beneath. Robinson created these collages using her diaries, notebooks, and research images and materials; her intention was to convey the "... messiness of death,... the disorder of the 'self'... after a great loss." And yet these collages are a very sweet synthesis. After the yearning for meaning from inanimate objects in the first section, and the frustrated need for a sensible gestural closure in the second, this final section is a repository for clarity and acceptance.

Robinson's use of both language and image confuses the distinction between object and subject. Her 'loss' is, simultaneously, her friend and a feeling that suffuses the objects around her. "Like a pair of binoculars with no right or wrong end, the camera makes exotic things near, intimate; and familiar things small, abstract, strange, much farther away." (Sontag 167).

In *a*, Robinson's text shouts out to the blank page. The photographs act as pools of contemplation amidst the human-reference of language; they take the burden of meaning from the objects and, finally, let them be.

> [. . .] I rise to say that my heart is only irritated OR a machine made frm human bones and a camera, [. . .] (30)

*Where are we and how can we think of ourselves as selves without death?*

Diane Ward

Los Angeles

------------

Works Cited:


Auster, Paul. "Introduction." *A Tomb for Anatole*.
    North Point Press, San Francisco: 1983.

Stéphane Mallarmé. *A Tomb for Anatole*. North Point
    Press, San Francisco: 1983.

Perloff, Marjorie. "The Difference is Spreading: on
    Gertrude Stein" in *American Poet*, 2000.
    http://www.poets.org/viewmedia.php/
    prmMID/19342. Accessed on 3/27/09.

Sontag, Susan. *On Photography*. Farrar, Straus, and
    Giroux, New York: 1973.

# Acknowledgements

Extracts from this book have been published in *The Reality Street Book of Sonnets,* ed. Jeff Hilson, 2008.

Thank you to Redell Olsen, Kristen Kreider and Robert Hampson at Royal Holloway for their help and advice.

& endless gratitude to Jude & Peter Davidson, my friends & my family for their kindness, love and support. This book is for Aerin, but it's also for all of you.

**Sophie Robinson** was born in 1985, and lives and works in London. She has an MA in Poetic Practice from Royal Holloway, University of London, and is currently researching a PhD in Queer Poetics. In 2006, she received the Phillipa Hicks award for Creativity and Innovation from the University of London, and her first chapbook, *Killin' Kittenish!* was published by yt communication in 2006. Her creative and critical work has also been published in *Pilot, How2, Dusie* and the *Openned anthology*.

**Caroline Bergvall** is an international writer and interdisciplinary poet working across media, languages, sonic and visual artforms. Recent works include *Alyson Singes* (Belladonna, 2008), *Cropper* (Torque Press, 2008), and *Fig* (Salt Books, 2005).

**Diane Ward** is the author of ten books of poetry, including *Flim-Yoked Scrim* (Factory School, 2006), *When You Awake* (Portable Press at Yo-Yo Labs, 2005), and *Portrait As If Through My Own Voice* (Margin to Margin, 2001).

**Ken Ehrlich** is an artist and writer based in Los Angeles. He has exhibited internationally in a variety of media, including video, sculpture and photography. He is the co-editor of *Surface Tension: Problematics of Site* (2003) and *Surface Tension Supplement No. 1* (2006) both published by Errant Bodies Press.

**Susan Simpson** is an experimental theater artist and filmmaker, and co-director of Automata. She has received grants from the Durfee Foundation, The California Community Foundation, Creative Capital, Multi- Arts Production Fund and is the 2002 recipient of the Center Theater Group's Richard E. Sherwood Award.

# TRENCHART Series of Literature

TRENCHART is an annual subscription series of new literature published by Les Figues Press. Each series includes five books situated within a larger discussion of contemporary aesthetics, as well as work by contemporary visual artists. All participants write an aesthetic essay or poetics; the first title in each series is the collection of these aesthetics, specially-bound in a limited-edition book available to subscribing members.

## TRENCHART: Tracer Series

*TrenchArt : Tracer*
aesthetics
ISBN 13: 978-1-934254-06-6

*A Fixed, Formal Arrangement*
Allison Carter
ISBN 13: 978-1-934254-07-3

*re: evolution*
Kim Rosenfield
ISBN 13: 978-1-934254-08-0

*I Go To Some Hollow*
Amina Cain
ISBN 13: 978-1-934254-09-7

*a*
Sophie Robinson
ISBN 13: 978-1-934254-10-3

Tracer Series Visual Artists: Ken Ehrlich & Susan Simpson

Become a subscribing member of Les Figues and receive all 5 titles in the TrenchArt Tracer Series.

Les Figues Press titles are available through:

Les Figues Press <http://www.lesfigues.com>
Small Press Distribution <http://www.spdbooks.org>

ƒ

**LES FIGUES PRESS**
Post Office Box 7736
Los Angeles, CA  90007
www.lesfigues.com
www.lesfigues.blogspot.com